Depression Recovery

According to

The Bible

Dr. Steven Waterhouse

Depression Recovery

According to

The Bible

First Edition 2008

Westcliff Press, P.O. Box 1521, Amarillo TX 79105
1-806-359-6362
email: westcliff@amaonline.com
www.webtheology.com

Ten Digit ISBN:0977405168
Thirteen Digit ISBN: 9780977405169

Printed in the United States of America

Suggested Cataloging-in-Publication Data

Waterhouse, Steven W.
   Depression Recovery According to the Bible
   48 Pages
   Includes Biblical References
   1. Pastoral Counseling 2. Depression, Mental – Religious Aspects
3. Suffering - Religious Aspects
   Suggested Library of Congress Number BV4012.2
   Suggested Dewey Number 253.5

Preface

This book is Dr. Waterhouse's revision of earlier research on the subject of depression. It was previously published in other resources that have been used by Westcliff Bible Church in its counseling and evangelistic ministry. This edition has been prepared especially at the request of **Sharing Hope**, which ministers to women in prisons across the United States.

The ministry of **Sharing Hope** is most appreciative of Dr. Waterhouse's efforts to provide this unique and comforting help for those who have particularly distressing personal needs. **Sharing Hope** would also like to thank Kimberly Lester for providing the cover design, as well as, her technical assistance in the production of this book.

April Riggs
Executive Director, Sharing Hope Ministries
P.O. Box 19985
Amarillo TX 79114

Depression Recovery

According to

The Bible

Stress and Self-Evaluation

Feelings of stress go with being human. The Bible presents life as a process of suffering before glory, just as the Lord Jesus Christ first suffered on the cross and then went to His crown in heaven. Having the "blues" from time to time is normal. As Romans 8:23 says, ..."we believers also groan ..."

If the alarm clock goes off and we do not feel exhilarated, this is not a serious problem. We should not expect to have constant highs in a fallen world. However, depression is more severe and needs attention. With depression the alarm clock goes off, and we can not face life. We can't sleep, or we sleep all the time. We can't eat, or we eat all the time.

The Bible gives at least 19 causes (and cures!) for our depression. Of course, the Bible also tells us how we can have contentment in life. Perhaps we feel so down we would skip its teachings on depression and move quickly to Bible verses on happiness. However, we will do better to discover what is wrong with us before considering the solution. A doctor will diagnose a sickness and only then prescribe medicine. No person ever has all 19 causes of depression. However, it is necessary to consider the entire list of causes before evaluating which apply to you. Many will not apply to you. However, by looking at all of them we will be careful not to overlook any possible root causes of your depression.

Look at Romans 12:3. What does this verse say?

_____

_____

We need not think we are perfect and have no problems. God already knows them and loves us anyway. As we now study possible causes of depression, let's have a reality check about self with a fair and "honest" evaluation.

*Is feeling stress normal?*_____

Why must a person consider all 19 causes of depression?

_____

Sinful Causes of Depression

I totally disagree with the conclusion that all depression arises from a person's own sin. Do not be afraid that this entire booklet will only be a long sermon on sin. However, it is a mistake to ignore sinful causes of depression. When people come to me for depression counseling, we always consider all 19 causes to be certain to get to the real problem. The Bible includes 11 sinful causes of depression. Upon reflection we can agree most of these are also common sense. To each cause of depression we only need to think of its opposite to find a solution.

1. Guilt – Solved by Forgiveness
Read Psalm 32.

In the Psalms King David speaks of depression. Phrases from Psalms 32 and 38 include: "I groaned all day long", "and I walk around filled with grief" and "my groanings come from an anguished heart." In Psalm 51:12 David prays that the joy of his salvation be restored.

David's depression had been caused by his adultery with Bathsheba and the cover-up that followed. Prior to his confession of sin, David grew more and more depressed. Guilt is to the soul what pain is to the body. The symptom of pain means we have a problem that needs attention. Likewise, guilt reveals we have a spiritual problem that needs attention. David said, "when I refused to confess my sin, my body wasted away and I groaned all day long" (Psalm 32:3-4). By contrast, David confessed his sins to God, and he returned to joy. In Psalm 51:7 he prayed "wash me, and I shall be whiter than snow."

All of us have sinned. God is a just Judge who can not just let sins go unpunished. However, the Holy Judge also loves us and does not want to punish us. He sent His Son, the Lord Jesus Christ, to die on the cross in our place. He paid our penalty and defeated death by rising again. When Christ died, our sins were placed on His moral and legal account. When a person trusts Him as Savior, His righteousness is transferred to the believer's account (or legal record).

God as Judge looks upon a believer in Christ as being cleansed from sin. Through faith in Christ as Savior, he or she stands "legally" before God uncondemned and acquitted. The Bible's term for this is "justification by faith." (See Romans 5:1, 9.)

If you have never placed your faith in Christ as Savior, guilt from unresolved sin is one of the hidden causes of your depression. The answer is to pray to God the Father and trust His Son as Savior. You can accept

His death on the cross as payment for sin. Then you need not feel guilt before God as Judge. Instead you will have Christ's righteousness transferred to your legal/moral standing before God. The answer to depression caused by guilt is "the joy of salvation."

How do we obtain forgiveness before God in His role as Judge? _____

Pain tells our body something is wrong just like the feeling of guilt tells our _____ that something is wrong.

What caused King David to suffer from depression? _____

Look at Psalm 32:5. What did King David finally do and what was the result? _____
_____

Do you see any area in your life that has unconfessed sin?
_____

2. Materialism – Solved by Contentment
Read 1 Kings 21:1-14.

Every advertisement is designed to make us feel discontentment. It is easy to buy into the world's philosophy that possessions will make us happy. Therefore, until we buy product X, Y, or Z we should feel unhappy with life.

The Bible gives the story of wicked King Ahab wanting to own Naboth's vineyard. The King had riches, but Naboth refused to sell his family farm for sentimental reasons. Because he could not buy the field, Ahab "went to bed with his face to the wall and refused to eat" (1 Kings 21:4).

Sometimes we are like Ahab. We believe buying something else will finally solve depression. In our times we often resort to "debt therapy" by putting purchases on credit cards. This can increase depression. However, even those with much money can become depressed. They keep buying more and more unnecessary products that can not fill emotional/spiritual emptiness in life.

The solution to depression caused by materialism involves a change of perspective. God has a perfect character. He gave us a perfect book. He has a loving and perfect plan for life. If we leave God, His Word and His will for life out of the picture, no material possession can make up the difference. Thinking that wealth alone can satisfy will lead to depression. Only God is perfect. All material things have flaws. The car gets scratched. The wardrobe fades.

This is not the same as concluding it is wrong to have nice things. The point is that possessions must be viewed as blessings from God not a substitute for God. If a person is already content with God as a primary source for satisfaction in life, then material things can secondarily be viewed as good blessings from God.

Yet, many of us try to ignore a perfect God and find happiness with imperfect consumer products. The Apostle Paul found contentment in the Lord Jesus Christ. Regarding material things he could be content with much (viewed as blessings from God) or content with little. "I have learned to be content with whatever I have. I know how to live on almost nothing or with everything ... This same God who takes care of me will supply all your needs ..." (Philippians 4:11-12, 19).

Will buying more things on credit cards solve depression?

*Do you think it is true that advertisements are designed to make us unhappy until we buy the product?*_____

Look at Philippians 4:11-13. Try to apply this verse to your life right now. _____

3. Anger – Solved by Confession, Entrusting Self to God
Read Genesis 4:1-16.

If we pause to reflect, we know from experience that anger often leads to depression. Anger seldom goes with joy in life.

The Bible tells the story of two brothers named Cain and Abel. Cain was the first murderer in human history. He killed his own brother. Genesis 4:5 has the phrase "This made Cain very angry and he looked dejected." In other words Cain's anger brought on depression. The next step in his downward spiral was Cain's violence against his innocent brother.

Anger may be the most complex emotion. Not all anger is wrong. Many have to read Ephesians 4:26 twice because it sounds like a misprint. This verse teaches "Be angry and yet do not sin" (NASB). We would think it should read "Be not angry." However, sometimes it is righteous to be angry. Things are not always fair or right. We might call this the "anger of God's honor." When God's holy standards for ethics are violated, we can become righteously angry. Yet, even in these situations Ephesians 4:26 commands us not to let this righteous anger lead to sin. Righteous anger can easily lead to hatred and an obsession for revenge. Instead righteous anger should be channeled into a search for understanding of why God allowed the wrong in my life. Non-sinful anger should also motivate us to work to change the world for the better.

The topic of righteous anger will come up later in this booklet under the topic of being a victim. For now we should move to sinful anger.

Some anger is righteous. We are mad when God's honor and standards have been trashed. However, the majority of anger is sinful. It is not anger over defending God's truths. Most anger is the "anger of self importance."

Righteous anger is slow and patient as is God's own anger over the wrongs in this world (see Psalm 103:8). Sinful anger flares up instantly over personal insults or impatience. Some of us are mad 24/7.

Seldom do we connect anger to depression. The Bible does. So does common sense. For our own emotional well being we must confess sinful anger to God as a sin. Many trivial insults and annoyances are not worth the resulting depression. A change in perspective as to whether the irritant is worth stewing in depression helps. Those who confess the anger of self-importance as sin and those who refuse stewing in anger over details will have far less depression. You may be thinking "my anger is righteous!" That may be true. A following section will take up the subject of handling injustice or being a victim of a serious evil. However, it is still true we must try to let go of as many burdens as possible. Even if the other person does not deserve it, we will have less depression if we take a pass on offenses of a secondary nature. They are not worth the constant agitation and depression. The Bible says, "People with understanding control their anger; a hot temper shows great foolishness" (Proverbs 14:29).

*What happened to Cain's emotions when he became angry and took it out on his brother?*_____

What does Proverbs 14:29 tell us about people who can't control their temper? _____

Is anger in the Bible always a sin? _____ *Explain how righteous anger can be used for good.* _____

As seen by the story of Cain, anger can lead to hatred and an obsession for revenge. Can you think of an example of this in your own life? _____

4. Hatred – Solved by Forgiveness, Love

The story of Jonah is best known for his adventure within the belly of the great fish. Instead of preaching to the people in Ninevah, Jonah went to sea to escape God's call. Jonah's reason for not wanting to go on the mission was not laziness. He hated the people of Nineveh. In the past they had attacked Israel, so it was fine with him if they never heard about salvation by faith in Israel's God. He wanted them to die and go to hell. In the final chapter of the book of Jonah, Jonah is depressed to the point of suicide. One would think a preacher would be depressed because of a lack of response to his message. No, in Jonah's case he was depressed because Nineveh repented and was saved. The words are amazing. "So he complained to the Lord about it: 'Didn't I say before I left home that you would do this, LORD? That is why I ran away to Tarshish! I knew that you are a merciful and compassionate God, slow to get angry and filled with unfailing love. You are eager to turn back from destroying people. Just kill me now, LORD! I'd rather be dead than alive if what I predicted will not happen'" (Jonah 4:2-3).

Why was Jonah so depressed that he preferred death to life? His amazing psychology was that he hated others so much it ruined his own life. Jonah was the case of a Jew who hated gentiles. Another Bible story connects depression with anti-Semitism.

The book of Esther tells the story of race hatred against the Jewish people. Haman was an evil tyrant who wanted to exterminate the Jews. Mordecai, Esther's relative, was a godly Jewish man. To this day Jewish people celebrate deliverance from Haman at the annual festival of Purim. Children dress in costumes and exchange gifts. Whenever the name of Haman is read in the ceremony Jewish boys and girls respond with a "hiss!" Haman told his wife he had "great wealth," he had "many children," he was "promoted" by the king above all others. However, all these advantages could not overcome depression. "But this is all worth nothing as long as I see Mordecai the Jew just sitting there at the palace gate" (Esther 5:13). Despite the blessings of life, Haman's hatred undid them all plunging him into depression.

It is a serious mistake to think good emotions can arise from hatred. Hatred brings depression whether the object is personally known or a vague unending hatred towards another people group. Jonah felt all gentiles should be damned. Haman felt all Jews should be dead. Both were depressed to the point of suicidal despair.

Jesus teaches to "love your enemies" Matt. 5:44. The Apostle Paul tells us to entrust any vengeance to God (Romans 12:19-20). The book of wisdom, Proverbs 20:22 advises, "Don't say 'I will get even for this wrong,' wait for the Lord, He will handle the matter."

God knows human psychology better than any expert. The less we hate, the better we feel.

Why was Jonah unhappy when the people of Nineveh responded to his message and were saved? _____

*Name two people in the Bible that were depressed because of hatred.*_____

*Read Matthew 5:44. God wants you to love your enemies. What else does he say that you should do?*_____

_____

*Read Romans 12:19-20. Paul tells us not to take revenge. What should we do instead based on these verses?*_____

_____

_____

*Can you think of anytime that you have hated someone so much that you felt depressed? What does God tell you to do about these feelings?*_____

_____

_____

5. Perfectionism - Solved by Acceptance of Human Limitations

   Some with perfectionist tendencies have unrealistic expectations of self or the world. Excellence is indeed a virtue. God wants us to achieve and work hard.

   However, God loves each of us without conditions. His love is not based on intelligence, appearance, talent, riches, or performance. All are made in the image of God. The Lord Jesus Christ loved you so much He died for you. If you will trust in Him as Savior, you become a child of God. God the Judge looks at believers as clothed in the righteousness of Christ. We already possess infinite value to God prior to any effort. Thus, the true motivation to achieve is not to find love and acceptance but because we are already precious to God.

Society has things totally backwards. It often bases our value on performance alone not on God's view of human value. Often society judges others by false and impossible standards. Can you think of a situation or a person where pleasing them would be totally impossible? If we base our sense of value upon what such people think of us, we will feel depressed. Yes, it is preferable to have people's approval; but it is more important to please God and derive our sense of value from God. The standards by which God measures life are accessible to all. They are either given by grace or attainable by anyone who wants to develop a character like Jesus. Our underlying value is not based on superficial things out of our control such as appearance, intelligence, talent or strength.

Moses is best known for the Ten Commandments. Yet, even Moses was so depressed by his perfectionist tendencies that he wanted to die. No matter how hard he worked the children of Israel simply would not follow God. His perfectionist tendencies led him to take responsibility for other people's disobedience. "I can't carry all these people by myself! . . . . go ahead and kill me" (Numbers 11:14-15).

We should let God's standards for value and excellence be the measure of our value and performance (not the world!). After pleasing God, we can have less worry or depression about being acceptable to others. It is also important to accept our human limitations. God does. We do not possess all beauty, strength, talent, or intelligence. He loves us the way we are. In one movie, a Catholic priest at Notre Dame tells a potential football player to consider two incontrovertible facts: "there is a God. I am not He." God knows human limitations. Striving to the point of depression is self-inflicted or society-inflicted. God loves us even within our limits. Excellence will please God, but He already loves us for who we are. We should strive for excellence as God defines excellence, but failure to enjoy God's acceptance and living by the world's perfectionist expectations produces depression. So does a refusal to accept our own human limits. "It is useless for you to work so hard from early morning until late at night, anxiously working for food to eat; for God gives rest to His loved ones" (Psalm 127:2).

Is God's love for us based upon our achievements or level of performance? _____

Even the great leader to whom God gave the Ten Commandments was not immune from depression. His name was _____.

What is the one way that we can strive to please God? ____
_____

If we are pleasing to _____, we can have less _____ about being acceptable to others.

6. Worry - Solved by Faith in God Instead
Read 1 Kings 19:1-4.

Everyone knows that worry and depression go together. The Biblical character Elijah illustrates this connection. After a victory over the false prophets of Baal, the wicked Queen Jezebel issues a death threat against the Lord's prophet, Elijah. She promises him death within 24 hours. Therefore, Elijah runs and the story continues with him sitting under a tree in the desert wanting to die. " ... Elijah was afraid and fled for his life . . . . and He sat under a solitary bloom tree, and he prayed that he might die. 'I've had enough, LORD.' he said, 'Take my life' " (1 Kings 19:3-4).

Have you ever been so fearful or worried that you wanted to die? If this can happen to Elijah, one of the most respected leaders in the entire Bible, then worry can drive any of us to depression even to thoughts of wanting to die. However, as the story continues, Elijah recovers from his depression. Of course, he needed rest because God told him "the journey ahead will be too much for you" (1 Kings 19:7). In a following section we will consider the link between medical problems (including exhaustion) and depression. For now, the main point is that Elijah's worries were cured by the presence of God. God was not in the whirlwind or earthquake. God was in the quiet.

The solution to worry (and the depression it may cause) is increased faith in God's presence and care in our lives. We typically find God in quiet Bible reading or prayer even more than the whirlwinds or the rocking quake of a big church event.

If you have never trusted in Jesus as Savior, there is indeed great cause to worry. By contrast, those who have faith in Christ as Savior have God's presence at all times and in all places. Hebrews 13:5 promises we need not fear because "I will never fail you. I will never abandon you." Since the care-taking Heavenly Father is always present, we can decrease our fears and decrease our depression. God watches over us and takes care of our needs. Psalm 42:5 shows that hope in God's presence, that is increased faith, has a direct relationship with overcoming depression based on worry. "Why am I discouraged? Why is my heart so sad? I will put my hope in God! I will praise him again – my Savior and my God."

It is true that we do need to do what we can about life's problems. The Bible allows what we might call "concern." If needs and problems cause us to have a level of worry that arises to "concern," this will not cause emotional problems. However, the Bible forbids us to worry at all about what might happen in the future. Jesus said we should handle each day one at a time but not worry about what *might* happen. "So don't worry about tomorrow ..." (Matthews 6:34). One good habit is to take life one day at a time solving the problems we can, leaving future and unsolvable problems to God. Several times the Bible pictures worry as a heavy weight that we cast off and let God carry for us. "Give your burdens to the LORD, and He will take care of you. He will not permit the godly to slip and fall" (Psalm 55:22). 1 Peter 5:7 teaches "give all your worries and cares to God, for he cares about you."

We should do what we can each day to face our problems, but we must refuse to worry about what might happen in the future or matters beyond our control. God promises that if we give Him prayer requests for such worries, "His peace will guard your hearts and minds" (see Philippians 4:6-7). This is a far better outcome than depression.

Read Hebrews 13:5. What does Jesus Christ promise?

_____

_____

Read Matthew 6:34. Summarize what this verse says about worry. _____

Is there a time that you worried about something that seemed overwhelming and out of your control? What have you learned that will help you when you experience depression from worry? _____

_____

7. Jealousy - Solved by Focusing on Exalting God
Read 1 Samuel 18:1-15.

Jealousy is a no-win emotion. When we are jealous, we will have depression. Sometimes jealousy deeply annoys the person we envy. Other times he or she could care less. Either way jealousy will make us depressed. Sometimes we might be jealous when another has obtained "success" unfairly or even by wickedness. Other times we might be envious of a person who obtained success honorably through virtue and hard work. With either type of situation, jealousy will lead to depression.

The most outstanding Bible example of envy towards a godly person would be Saul's jealousy of David. Saul was king. The Philistine giant Goliath challenged Israel to send a representative to combat. David killed Goliath with a sling and cut off his head. Here is an example of a righteous person having success. Would this not be a basis for joy? Of course, most of Israel was happy that an honorable person had success. They danced in the streets. Yet, King Saul grew jealous when he heard a chant that compared him to David. "Saul has killed thousands, and David his ten thousands" (1 Samuel 18:7). Saul's reaction was immediate jealousy followed by depression. "This made Saul very angry. 'What's this?' he said. 'They credit David with ten thousands and me with only thousands'" (1 Samuel 18:8). For the rest of his life Saul was jealous of David and for the rest of his life Saul was deeply depressed. He ultimately fell on his own sword committing suicide.

Why should we ever be jealous of a good hard-working person who has success? If he or she is a good person living to glorify God, should we not wish him to make progress? All jealousy does is make us depressed.

Almost everyone can agree that envy directed at a good person is unreasonable. More difficult are situations involving jealousy against people who succeed despite or even because of being evil. This seems so unfair. God's Word agrees that life can be unfair in the short term. Sometimes wicked people seem to get ahead. However, there is more to evaluate than just the short term. No one should envy the wicked that prosper. God only allows this for a brief time. There is absolutely no need to be jealous when the wicked achieve. We would not want to exchange places when they have their downfall. If we become jealous of the wicked, it makes little more sense than envying the good. Furthermore, it still causes depression.

The following passages in the Psalms tell us how to view wicked people who advance, certainly not with envy. These Bible texts remind there is no need to be jealous of wicked people when we consider their final end.

"Do not worry about the wicked, or envy those who do wrong. For like the grass, they soon fade away. Like spring flowers, they soon wither. Trust in the LORD and do good. Then you will live safe in the land and prosper. Take delight in the LORD, and he will give you your heart's desires. Commit everything you do to the LORD. Trust him, and he will help you" (Psalm 37:1-5).

"But as for me, I almost lost my footing. My feet were slipping, and I was almost gone. For I envied the proud when I saw them prosper despite their wickedness" . . . . "If I had really spoken this way to others, I would have been a traitor to your people. So I tried to understand why the wicked prosper. But a difficult task it is! Then I went into your sanctuary, O God, and I finally understood the destiny of the wicked" (Psalm 73:2-3, 15-17).

Jealousy arises from an obsession with self. Less self promotion leads to less jealousy and then to less depression. We will have more joy if we concentrate instead on God's character, promises, and teaching in the Bible. If a person's goal in life is to honor self above all else, there will be jealousy and depression. If instead we focus on God's honor, then indirectly personal blessings will be a result but without depression. Those who keep their minds on God's exaltation can expect God to give them honor and success in some way and at some time. There is a difference between purpose and result. If we purpose to honor God, God promises this will result in self-honor. "I will honor those who honor Me" (1 Samuel 2:30). With this mindset, there is absolutely no need for jealousy. If we focus on honoring God and let Him worry about honoring self (which He promises He will), then we never have need of jealousy, and can escape any depression from it (see also Psalm 75:6-7; Jeremiah 9:23-24; 1 Corinthians 4:7).

Instead of stewing in jealousy when an evil person seems to have success, we should do what? _____

_____

Read 1 Samuel 2:30. If we honor God, we need not be jealous because God promises to honor those who

_____

Can you think of someone who you have been jealous of? How did that make you feel? Read Jeremiah 9:23-24. Summarize what this verse says to you. _____

_____

_____

8. Laziness - Solved by Well-Being from Productivity –
Read Ecclesiastes 3:22.

An earlier section warned about overworking to the point of perfection. However, sometimes people are lazy. Lazy people are seldom content. In fact laziness and depression go together. The Bible does list hard work as one of the curses resulting from sin (Genesis 3:17-19). However, God planned for Adam and Eve to work in Paradise even before the fall. Part of the image of God within people includes being creative as God is the Creator. Everyone is different. Some people create by cooking recipes. Others create by building highways or houses. Some write music, poems, sermons, or books. If we find productive and righteous pursuits that fit our own aptitude and personal design by God, we will have less depression. Ecclesiastes 3:13 calls labor "the gift of God." Later in the chapter Solomon advises that we "should be happy" in activities (Ecclesiastes 3:22). We should make the most of opportunities in life within the limitations of our circumstances (play the cards that have been dealt). Everyone with reflection can think of things to do that are beneficial to growth (reading, exercising, singing, writing, developing work skills that are interesting to the individual, participating in church/civic programs). Work and creativity reduce depression.

Are lazy people happy people? _____

What are some ways that you can enjoy being creative as God made us to be? _____

9. Rejection of Christ - Solved by Faith in Christ as Savior
Read Matthew 27:1-5

Judas betrayed Jesus. Then he "went out and hanged himself" (Matthew 27:5). The Lord Jesus Christ is the foundational source for joy in life. It is impossible to leave Him out of life and end with happy results.

One time a doctor came to me for serious depression counseling. She made over $750,000 a year and was still extremely depressed. She asked if she could get better without accepting Christ as Savior. My reply was that she could improve from her suicidal level but never to the point of true happiness. Later I will finish her story. The truth for now is that no amount of humanistic advice for depression can overcome our spiritual needs. Those who reject or are indifferent to the Lord Jesus Christ will experience unavoidable depression for which there is no alternative answer.

Can those who reject the Lord Jesus Christ as Savior ever completely overcome depression? _____

10. Sex as god - Solved by Viewing Sex as God's Gift
Read 1 Corinthians 7:3-5.

Almost no one would say sex is their god, but many do in fact worship sex. God created us male and female with the intention of a blessing (almost the very wording of Genesis 1:27). The Bible views sexuality as a core and beneficial part of human nature. When practiced within the safety of a lifelong marriage commitment, sexual experiences are a great gift from God. The entire book of Song of Solomon praises marital intimacy, as well as, other Bible texts such as Proverbs 5:18-19, 1 Corinthians 7:3-5, and Hebrews 13:4.

Everything in the Bible that is holy is also restricted. The Holy of Holies in the Jewish Temple was restricted to only the high priest. Separation is a characteristic of holiness. Because the marriage bed is holy, God restricts it to only those who have made a covenant (marriage vows).

Another function of restriction is safety. God intends sexuality to be fun within the boundaries of safety. His commandments are not to destroy fun but for our well-being. Suppose we build a fence around the playground of an elementary school. The fence is not to destroy fun. The barrier keeps the children from wandering off into the streets and being harmed. Within the playground of complete safety, the school kids can have all the fun they want. Within the boundary of marriage a couple is not only allowed but also commanded by the Bible to enjoy each other. By contrast, what some foolishly misdefine as "fun" is really a form of self-harm. God's restrictions on sex actually preserve "fun."

By leaving God out of life, many also have the tragic misconception that sexual experiences alone will give meaning to life. Instead of interest and focus on the genuine God, they think some type of sex will give meaning to life that only can come from God. The proper view is that only God can be God. Husbands, wives, and sexuality within marriage should be viewed as a gift and blessing from God but not a replacement for God. We may legitimately view sex as God's gift to humanity, but those who worship it, not God, end up with psychological and/or emotional problems including depression. Because sex can not fill the emptiness that only God can fill and because sexual experiences outside the limits of safety are so devastating, there can result a cycle of worsening depression. One may think happiness or the meaning of life is just around the corner with the next partner or a new position or an ever-increasing experimentation that can even lead to perversion. All of this will only increase depression. The new man or woman, the new method, even the new perversion fails to meet our inner needs just as previous failures. The way out of this destructive spiraling mess is to confess sexual sins to God for cleansing. Then adopt His teachings on this most vital aspect to humanity. God wants us to view Him as the ultimate reason to live. Then we should wait on His plan in finding another Christian to marry.

Most people do not make a connection between depression and an out of control sexuality. Yet, isn't this just common sense for anyone who would stop and think? The Bible gives an example of destructive sex leading to depression. The story is not well known because it just recounts the history of a twisted and sick person. This is the sort of story that does not make the selection as appropriate bed-time reading for children. In 2 Samuel 13 Prince Amnon, David's son, develops an infatuation with his half-sister, Tamar. He believes he can only find happiness if he can conquer his half-sister. His twisted obsession makes him miserable. His friend asks, "What's the trouble? Why should the son of a king look so dejected (depressed) morning after morning?" (2 Samuel 13:4). His reply is that he can not possibly find happiness in life without possessing his half-sister. Later he raped her and plunged into deeper depression.

This unfamiliar ancient story parallels contemporary common behavior. People get themselves into depression lusting for a different or new experience they think will finally make them happy. If they follow through and fulfill the act, it never works. The result is even greater frustration (depression).

Sex is good if within the boundaries of emotional (and medical) safety. Sex is God's gift. Yet, sex can not replace God in meeting all our deepest needs. Worshiping sex as a god and at the same time rejecting God is a certain path to frustration (depression).

What does the Bible say about sexuality within marriage?

_____

Do you agree or disagree with the point that some people regard sex as a substitute "god", misusing it to meet deeper needs?

_____

Who is the one who can meet all our deepest needs? _____

Have you had relationships in the past where you had the wrong view of sex? How did those relationships end? Can you see where depression could occur in a relationship that was outside of God's plan for sex? _____

11. Occult - Solved by Rejection of Satan

The main draw to Satan worship is the promise of power. If one feels weak and vulnerable, there is a temptation to join groups that promise power either from joining a gang or the offer of supernatural magic, hexes on enemies, or even love spells on others.

Occult involvement promises power but gives slavery and depression. The Bible makes an obvious tie between the occult and depression. Saul's great depression came when God allowed an evil spirit to bother him (1 Samuel 16:14). His greatest foolishness was to consult a witch (1 Samuel 28). His depression continued, and eventually he killed himself (1 Samuel 31).

God is the source of human joy. Satan is the complete opposite. To overcome depression we must reject the slavery of the occult.

At this point in the booklet we have considered 11 sources of depression which may be classified as sinful. Many of them involve attention upon self only, with no attention upon God, the source of joy. To overcome these problems, we can and must reverse them. No one alone can do so, but through God all these problems have answers. To defeat depression we must choose: forgiveness from God (not guilt), contentment with God (not materialism), entrusting all wrongs to God (not anger), love (not hatred), faith in God (not worry), honoring God, leaving our time and way of personal honor up to

Him (not jealousy), productivity (not laziness), accepting Christ (not rejection of the source of joy), viewing sex as God's gift (not as a substitute god), and rejection of Satan (not depression from slavery to him).

Beyond these 11 sinful causes of depression, the Bible gives eight more non-sinful causes of depression. It is perhaps best to sub-divide these by treating false ideas and medical causes of depression separately.

*Now is a good time to review the sinful causes of depression. Can you see where any of these are true in your life?*_____

Non-Sinful Causes of Depression

Even though a person does nothing to bring about the non-sinful causes of depression, he or she must still face such problems in order to recover.

1. Being a Victim of Sin - Solved by Refusal to be a Lifelong Victim
Read Exodus 6:6-9.

The Bible gives two outstanding examples of victimization by others leading to depression. Before God used Moses to deliver Israel from slavery in Egypt, the Pharaoh was oppressing the Hebrew slaves. Logically, the book of Exodus says this mistreatment caused severe "discouragement" (that is depression), see Exodus 6:9. A second example is the Lord Jesus Christ who was the world's ultimate victim. Being God He has all power and all knowledge. He is present everywhere at the same time. Yet, being also human He suffered greatly.

He Himself did no sin. Yet, all our sins were laid on Him (Isaiah 53:6). This means in a legal sense the guilt of our sin was transferred to His account. Then He paid for our sins and rose again. He will give freely His righteous standing to all who trust Him and His death on the cross as a substitute payment for the penalty of sin.

The Lord Jesus Christ never sinned, but He can relate to anyone who is the victim of sin, ranging from insult to violence. The night before the cross Jesus in His human nature grew depressed over the pending victimization. "My soul is crushed with grief to the point of death" (Matthew 26:38).

A child abandoned by mother or father, a husband or wife whose spouse commits adultery, or a crime victim will have a natural tendency toward depression.

The solution to depression arising from a moral offense is forgiveness. I can now imagine a reader thinking, "You do not know how badly I have been wronged. Forgiveness is difficult or impossible for the evil against me." Let me encourage you to continue reading. In the end forgiveness to reduce depression will make perfect sense.

Forgiveness has more than one emphasis. This is best considered from an analysis of "unforgiveness." To withhold forgiveness could mean to hate and seek personal revenge. Yet, to withhold forgiveness might also refer to holding another personally accountable. The first shade of meaning involves emotions. The second involves justice. Years ago one of the youth in our church stole $100.00 from the church offering. The church board immediately forgave in the sense of dropping hatred and seeking revenge. However, we did withhold forgiveness in the sense of moral accountability. He was required to apologize to the donor (whose check he had stolen) and to replace the money. In reality moral accountability was beneficial to the young man who learned from his mistake.

When a person is wronged, he or she has several options according to the Bible. If a wrong can be classified in a relatively minor category such as a snub or an insult, it is best to give total forgiveness even if the offender never apologizes. Proverbs 19:11 says, "sensible people control their temper, they earn respect by overlooking wrongs." 1 Peter 4:8 says, " ... love covers a multitude of sins." Notice the verse does not say "love covers all sins." However, a majority of times we can overlook the offense. Often the wrong simply is not worth any negative emotional impact. If we can in good conscience overlook the matter, we should. There will be less depression if we try not to let small offenses bother our hearts and minds. As much as we can, we should classify as many offenses as possible in the "overlook" category. While the wrongdoer does not deserve such grace, the one being wronged will overcome depression by refusing to stew mentally over the small stuff. Of course, the term "sin" covers many degrees of wrong. Sometimes the offense is far too serious for us to just let pass in forgiveness defined as dropping accountability.

Even in these most serious situations, God wants us to forgive in the sense of dropping hatred and revenge. Jesus said, "...love your enemies" (Matthew 5:44). Hatred and vengeance will not change the offender. It will cause us to be depressed. Even when they were killing Him, Jesus said, "Father, forgive them, for they don't know what they are doing" (Luke 23:34, see other verses on forgiveness in Mark 11:25 and Romans 12:17-20).

In situations involving serious offenses, we should still always relinquish hatred because of what the hatred does to us. It makes us miserable and depressed and takes the focus off the blessings and perfections of God.

Nevertheless, while it is good psychology always to forgive in the sense of avoiding hatred, the Bible does not always command us to forgive in the sense of dropping moral accountability. While it is always right and emotionally best to forgive in the sense of rejecting vengeance and hatred, we do have the option of holding another accountable. The Bible allows us to go in private and seek apology (Matthew 18:15-17). For serious offenses church leaders can withdraw membership for an offender. When a wrong reaches a criminal category, it is not wrong to seek redress from the courts (Romans 13:4).

When we are wronged, holding another accountable need not cause depression. The Bible permits us to speak up about a serious evil and to hold others accountable.

Suppose one decides that an offense is too serious to overlook but attempts at reconciliation and/or justice fail. We go to the person and seek an apology, but he or she does not care to reconcile. We go to the courts, but justice is not served. How shall we end the matter?

The Bible permits attempts to hold another accountable in cases where the offense is just too serious to overlook.   However, if such attempts fail, we must ultimately turn frustration and heartbreak over to God. Jesus did. He was a serious victim. Justice for Him took place in heaven not earth. If at the end, you have been seriously wronged without any apology or fair settlement, it is wise to turn the whole mess over to God. He alone will ensure justice in His time. Those who follow Jesus' example will have far less depression.

"For God called you to do good, even if it means suffering, just as Christ suffered for you. He is your example, and you must follow in his steps. He never sinned, nor ever deceived anyone. He did not retaliate when he was insulted, nor threaten revenge when he suffered. He left his case in the hands of God who always judges fairly" (1 Peter 2:21, 23).

How did Jesus become the Bible's ultimate victim resulting in sympathy for all who have been wronged?

Is it wrong to hold another accountable for a serious wrong?

How should we respond when no apology or fair settlement over a wrong ever happens? _____

2. False Guilt - Solved by Biblical Standards of Right and Wrong

False guilt refers to guilt feelings that arise when no actual sin has been committed. Several factors may produce false guilt including accidents, legalism, or choosing not to accept or enjoy God's complete forgiveness. Each of these types of false guilt can lead to depression. Each has a different solution.

False guilt often comes after a mistake, accident, or stressful decision. One lady I counseled felt depression after a car accident in which the other driver died. Another felt false guilt over the tough decision to place a relative in a nursing home. Sometimes, children whose parents divorce endure false guilt by blaming themselves. 1 John 3:20 is a good Bible verse for occasions of false guilt from accidents or situations beyond human control. "Even if we feel guilty, God is greater than our feelings, and he knows everything." Feeling guilt for mishaps or situations beyond our control is false. God would not blame us for such things.

A second type of false guilt arises from man-made rules that are not even in the Bible. Christians call this legalism. When a leader or group goes beyond the Bible to make up rules, we may feel guilt for not keeping them.

Yet, such guilt is false. If the rule or practice is not required by the Bible, then at most it is a matter of group policy or personal preference, not Christian ethics. Even churches can judge each other by matters that are strictly speaking not a matter of right and wrong (styles of music or dress at church services, which Bible translation to use). When the Bible does not clearly teach on a moral point (as by contrast, lying, stealing, adultery, murder), God often allows diversity in matters of taste and culture. Guilt over breaking such practices is not true guilt but false guilt. The solution for false guilt is a study of what the Bible itself actually defines as a sin and not letting man- made rules cause depression.

A third type of false guilt arises when we continue to hang on to our guilt even after God has forgiven us. When a person trusts in Jesus as Savior, he or she is completely forgiven before God as Judge. Colossians 2:13 says, "... he forgave all our sins." This means a Christian need not feel depressed concerning his or her standing before God the Judge. God does not lie. A believer is cleansed from all sin by trusting in the Lord Jesus Christ.

After faith in Christ, we become related to God as Father. The believer is forgiven by God the *Judge* by faith alone for all sins past and future. However, even a saved person (whose destiny is in heaven) can still sin and needs forgiveness before God as *Father.* There is no need to be saved again (or over and over) because we are forgiven by God the *Judge* on the basis of faith alone. However, a Christian gains forgiveness from the Heavenly Father by confession of sin. In the Lord's Prayer a Christian asks the Father to "forgive us our sins" (Luke 11:4). John teaches, "But if we confess our sins to him, he is faithful and just to forgive us our sins and to cleanse us from all wickedness" (1 John 1:9). After faith in Christ or a believer's confession of sin to God in prayer, remaining guilt feelings are false guilt. Instead we should believe

God's promises that we are now clean from sin. Failure to accept and believe God's promises of forgiveness leads to unnecessary false guilt. The Apostle Paul had persecuted Christians to the point of being a murderer prior to his conversion. He could have made excuses for wallowing in false guilt. Instead he refused any false guilt by accepting God's forgiveness. He viewed life as a race and refused to look back. Forgiven sins were left in the past as he looked above to heaven and forward to the future. "... Forgetting the past and looking forward to what lies ahead ..." (Philippians 3:13). You and I must have the same perspective on past sins to avoid false guilt with its resulting depression.

What are the three types of false guilt that were listed?

_____

What does 1 John 3:20 say about feelings of false guilt?

_____

Paul persecuted Christians to the point of being a murderer. Review Philippians 3:13-14. Summarize what Paul wrote in these verses. _____

_____

Have you ever felt false guilt over accidents or not accepting God's complete forgiveness? Explain. _____

_____

What Bible verse is good for false guilt? _____

3. Rejection, Betrayal, Unfair Criticism - Solved by Security in God's Love

Those who have been betrayed by others (such as abandonment by a spouse, parent, or friend) and those who have experienced unfair criticism will likely face depression. Of course, this is not a deliberately chosen course of events. We may indeed be innocent, but the broken relationship or meanness still can lead to depression.

In the Bible King David faced a political rebellion from his own son, Absalom. When fleeing Jerusalem for his life, David did not even care when his enemies cursed and cast down stones from ledges on the side of the road (2 Samuel 16). This indicated extreme depression rising from his son's betrayal.

You may have experienced a similar treachery in the past or unfair criticism. In Numbers 11, the people criticized Moses as a leader. They actually wanted to return to slavery in Egypt rather than continue to follow Moses. This unfair criticism was another factor in Moses' request to God, "just go ahead and kill me ..." (Numbers 11:15). Like David or Moses, rejection or betrayal by others can cause serious depression. How can we avoid this?

We must focus attention, hopes and security upon the Lord Jesus Christ. Others may fail us. They might later renew the relationship, but often they fail us permanently and never come back. Yet, the Lord Jesus Christ promises "I will never fail you. I will never abandon you" (Hebrews 13:5). He remains loyal and will never reject believers (see John 6:37).

The Lord Jesus Christ can not relate to sin, but He can sympathize with rejection. "He was despised and rejected" (Isaiah 53:3). He "understands our weakness" (Hebrews 4:15) because He knows the heart break of depression arising from being rejected.

Jeremiah was another godly person who experienced much rejection. He is known as "the weeping prophet" because he faithfully preached God's truth for forty years and virtually everyone rejected him. He overcame rejection by focus on a perfect God (Jeremiah 9:23-24) and a perfect book (the Bible, Jeremiah 15:15-17). As long as God approved his life what others thought of him was unimportant.

Psalm 109 contains some interesting phrases for when others reject or harshly criticize. "Let them curse me if they like, but you [God] will bless me!" (Psalm 109:28). "For He [God] stands beside the needy to save them from those who condemn them" (Psalm 109:31). We can paraphrase these thoughts: "As long as God blesses, the curses by enemies do not matter" and "God will stand by you when others judge you unfairly."

Focusing on the loyalty of the Lord Jesus Christ, the perfections of God, and the Bible help to get us through rejection and criticism. It will also help to find Christian friends who will never reject us because they have learned to treat people as Christ does.

*Have you ever experienced betrayal or unfair criticism which led to depression?*_____

The Lord Jesus can sympathize with us when we experience betrayal. Isaiah 53:3 says, "He was _____and _____of men."

What can we do when we are unfairly rejected, betrayed or criticized? _____

4. Broken Dreams - Solved by a Motivation to Glorify God, Leaving the Results to Him

I do not disagree at all with the advice to have lofty goals and dreams for life. Striving for a noble vision helps produce great results. Even if the goal is not quite obtainable perfectly, more progress will be made by having a dream and making an attempt.

Yet, unrealized dreams can lead to depression. Some dreams fail to materialize. A person may fail to make the Olympic team despite years of sacrificial training. After long hours of hard and stressful labor a business may still fail. A pastor may preach a wonderful sermon but few respond. A soldier may completely fulfill his or her duty but lose his or her life.

None of these examples cancel out the truth of the old song "to dream the impossible dream." We must continue to hope and to try, but we must add a Christian perspective on life in order to have the courage to try great things without risking depression. There is no greater motivation in life than to glorify God. When we dream great things and attempt great things, we can always succeed if the underlying standard is to honor God. We can always succeed in honoring God even if we come only half way in realizing some of our big dreams. To hear God say "well done" (Matthew 25:21 and 23) is real success. Coming up short in a worthy goal is still better than quitting.

David dreamed about building a great temple in Jerusalem. Because David had killed so many in past battles, God chose Solomon, David's son, to build the Temple. David's greatest dream for life never happened, but God still blessed him. David's dream failed, but God still said "...your intention is good ..." (2 Chronicles 6:8). We are better off having a vision of excellence and striving towards great dreams. However, if the deepest motive is to honor God in life, we can still be a success, even if we do not obtain everything we hope or plan. King David's dream failed, but he succeeded in honoring God. He did not build the Temple, but he obtained just as great an honor because he was "a man after God's own heart" (1

Samuel 13:14; Acts 13:22). Dream big, but honor God above the goal. Then there is always success without risk of depression.

Explain how David failed in his dream but still honored God. _____

Is it good to aim at the "impossible dream?" _____

What greater goal in life guarantees success even if we experience broken dreams? _____

5. Trying to Please Everyone - Solved by Living By God's Standards First

God's Word is the measure of virtue and excellence. His commands are neither unreasonable nor a burden (see Matthew 11:28, 30, 1 John 5:3). When we obey and please God, many righteous people will encourage us.

However, many people do not evaluate others by God's standards. They can have self-created standards for judging others that are unfair and/or unrealistic. Outside of deeply spiritual Christians, the world can be totally lacking a gracious and loving attitude.

Grace involves tolerating other people's flaws. The Bible teaches us to make allowances for other people's faults and to forgive (Colossians 3:13; Ephesians 4:2). Often crabby people are really upset with God or insecure or have problems unrelated to the person they attack in their misdirected venting. They can be harsh critics. Trying to please fussy people can cause depression. They impose impossible expectations on us.

This can happen in any situation such as church or the workplace. The Bible verse that most proves that trying to please everyone will cause depression concerns the family. Colossians 3:21 tells fathers not to be overly demanding and critical of children. "Fathers do not aggravate your children, or they will become discouraged." The principle of "discouragement" (or depression) from trying to please unreasonable people can be transferred to areas beyond the family. Often those with the most loyal hearts are the very ones most depressed by trying to meet the unreasonable expectations of others.

We do need to concentrate on pleasing God by keeping the commandments that are in the Bible. Beyond this, however, we may need to set limits upon efforts to satisfy others. Pleasing God should lead to the approval of most people. If not, we should refuse to worry about judgmental people and decide not to let unreasonable critics ruin our emotions. Titus 2:15 says, "don't let anyone disregard what you say." There are limits to what we have to take from others. This does not mean we take revenge, but we must adjust our attitudes to realize when we obey God first, it does not matter whether others approve or not.

Have you ever experienced depression from trying to please everyone? _____

We do need to concentrate on _____ *God first.*

6. Loneliness - Solved by Fellowship with God and People

1 Kings 19 tells the story of Elijah sitting under a tree wanting to die. His depression arose from several factors. Among them was loneliness. "I am the only one left ..." (1 Kings 19:10). Later God tells Elijah he certainly was not the only one who still followed God (verse 18). Like Elijah we all tend to be depressed by loneliness. Also, like Elijah no one is really alone. God is the ultimate friend. For those who have faith in Christ as Savior, God

is always present. He both dwells within and is present at all times around a believer. "I will never fail you. I will never abandon you" (Hebrews 13:5).

In addition, it is usually possible to find other believers who can be trusted as friends. Participation in an assembly of believers for worship, instruction, and fellowship causes Christians to "encourage one another" (Hebrews 10:25). This counters depression from loneliness.

Read and summarize Hebrews 10:25. _____

_____

Do the people that you surround yourself with offer encouragement? If not, list ways that you can surround yourself with believers that can encourage you. _____

_____

To this point we have considered 11 sinful causes of depression and 6 non-sinful causes: being a victim of sin, false guilt, broken dreams, rejection or betrayal by others, trying to please everyone and loneliness. To counter these contributors to depression we should: refuse to be a lifelong victim, follow biblical standards of right and wrong, gain security in God's love, glorify God and leave results to Him, live to please God first and then not worry about people, and look to God and Christians for friendship.

Two more causes for depression are also non-sinful, but they may be better classified separately. False ideas cause depression, and medical problems cause depression.

Please read again the list of the non-sinful causes of sin and steps to counter them.

False Ideas – Solved by Truth

Thinking affects emotions. What we believe influences how we feel. Often people are unaware that their depression stems from a false worldview and assumptions.

The typical humanist mindset alone is sufficient to bring on depression. Earlier we mentioned an affluent lady doctor who suffered with serious depression because of her rejection of Christ as Savior. I asked her if she believed in evolution or creation. She said "evolution." I said "How can you avoid depression if you believe you are a birth defect from slime? That is extremely depressive thinking." Next I asked if she believed in life after death. She said, "I am unsure." I said, "Here is a second depressive false idea." False ideas can produce bad emotions including depression. Most unbelievers never make the connection between the world's mixed-up ideas and depression.

Sometimes parental failures lead to false ideas that bring depression. Ideally, we should develop our image of God from the way parents treat us. God is always present. He knows everything. He has all power. He is eternal. He treats us with holiness, grace, and love.

Good parents are still imperfect, but they model God's traits to their children. To a small child parents seem present for every need. They have all the answers, great power, and have lived what seems to be forever. They insist on right and wrong, but they also give grace and unconditional love. In families with such parents, the children understand God by parental attitudes and actions long before they are old enough to read about the Heavenly Father in Scripture. Those who grow up in such homes have an easier time viewing God's real character.

Yet, many today have a disadvantage because their mother or father or both did not resemble God even in an approximate way. While this can be overcome, those from dysfunctional homes have a harder time realizing God is not a tyrant. While He is holy, His grace and unconditional love have been expressed by sending His Son to provide forgiveness. Accepting salvation by faith in Christ should lead to the view that God loves us eternally. A biblical view of God's image will lesson depression as opposed to thinking of a distorted image of God displayed by parents or taught by confused preachers.

In addition to a false image of God derived from poor examples, depression can arise from false teaching about salvation. The Bible teaches eternal life is a gift given by grace through faith. "...the free gift of God is eternal life" (Romans 6:23). "God saved you by his grace when you believed ...it is a gift from God" (Ephesians 2:8-9). Falsely thinking we must work to earn salvation leads many to depression. We must work to please God and have greater rewards in heaven, but eternal life itself is a gift through faith alone.

The typical "prosperity gospel" could also cause depression. God promises to supply our needs (Philippians 4:19), and God wants us to ask for health when we are fearful (Philippians 4:6), but it goes beyond the Bible's authority to conclude that God promises prosperity and health to all. Jesus was homeless and poor (Matthew 8:20; 2 Corinthians 8:9). Even Paul's prayers for health were sometimes denied (2 Corinthians 12:7-9). Thinking God guarantees there can never be sickness or promises us riches goes beyond the Bible's promises for this life and can cause depression.

Bad theology produces bad psychology including depression. False ideas such as evolution, the denial of life after death, false views of an unloving and unforgiving God, salvation by works, and the "prosperity" gospel; are just some examples. The solution to false ideas is careful Bible study to determine truth. Most people are unaware of the connection between thinking and feeling. Good theology produces good psychology including peace of mind not depression.

What false ideas from the non-Christian world lead to depression? _____

Bad _____ *produces bad* _____ *including depression.*

Good _____ *produces good* _____ *including peace.*

Should we trust everything that people tell us about God? _____. *The solution is to carefully study the* _____ *to determine the truth.*

Medical Depression – Solved by Healthy Lifestyle, Medicine

A conservative approach to using medicine for depression is wise. A rejection of even the possibility of medicine is not.

Non-Christian counselors tend to overlook the many spiritual, emotional, or relational causes of depression and think only of medicine. Then sometimes the person is still depressed because the root causes were neglected. Assuming there is no risk of suicide, it seems better to consider first all the possible factors contributing to depression before using medicine. If these spiritual or emotional factors can be ruled out and one has also tried a healthy lifestyle, then medicine may well be necessary.

Some depression is medical in origin. Exhaustion was a primary factor in Elijah's depression. Rather than giving a counseling session, the angel of the Lord told Elijah, "Get up and eat some more, or the journey ahead will be too much for you ..." (1 Kings 19:7). Psalm 102 gives the prayer of a sick person. Verse four says, "My heart is sick, withered like grass, and I have lost my appetite."

Once I counseled with a "cowboy" type man for depression. None of the previous 18 causes of depression seemed to fit. However, he told me he woke up every morning at 4:00AM to drive many miles to work in the oilfields. He always worked overtime and had not taken time for vacation in over ten years. As with Elijah, this man was a case of burnout causing depression.

If none of the preceding causes of depression seem to fit, the problem may well be exhaustion or another medical problem. When we need medicine, we should not feel any false guilt. Yet, those who need medicine still need God. Medicine might help restore clear thinking, but only the Lord Jesus Christ can give a satisfying life (John 10:10).

What Bible story illustrates a medical problem contributing to depression? _____
_____

Have you ever felt that you had an unhealthy lifestyle that could cause depression? What are some things that you could change to help overcome this? _____
_____

Those who need medicine still _____
_____

Time to Evaluate and Improve

The Bible has much more to teach about depression than most people realize. No one will have all the various causes of depression, but most of us have a few of them. Because we often lack insight into our own needs, it is important to consider the complete list and select those that apply. You must ask yourself, "Which of these biblical causes of depression are true in my life?" This will only benefit if there is an honest evaluation before God. If you can identify the problems, then give special attention to reviewing those sections of this booklet.

Most biblical causes of depression also have something to do with neglecting or forgetting God and concentrating only on self. Depression logically results from neglecting God because God is the source of joy. We all need to focus on the perfect God as the source for meaning and satisfaction in life (not self or a seriously flawed world system or disappointing people, possessions, or experiences).

Various Bible texts do lend support to the idea that comedy (Proverbs 17:22), music (1 Samuel 16:16, 23), and the choice to think positive not negative thoughts help with depression (Philippians 4:8-9). These have value because they give attention to God by music and meditation. God also created humans to laugh.

Those who remain indifferent and neglectful of God will have depression. If we continue to praise Him, think about Him, and seek Him, we will also be finding contentment and peace, the opposite of depression.

"The LORD is my strength and my song" (Exodus 15:2).

"The joy of the LORD is your strength"   (Nehemiah 8:10).

" ... for I rejoice in the LORD" (Psalm 104:34).

"You will keep in perfect peace, all who trust in you, all whose thoughts are fixed on you ... " (Isaiah 26:3).

"Always be full of joy in the Lord. I say it again – rejoice!" (Philippians 4:4).

After finishing this booklet, can you identify causes of depression that are true in your life? _____

The way to God the Father is by His Son, the Lord Jesus Christ. Have you placed faith in Christ as your Savior in order to be right with God, the real source of contentment and peace? If not, please look over the steps for becoming a Christian.

To become a Christian a person must first realize that he or she is "lost" (separated from God as the result of personal sin). Look up the following Scriptures in your Bible in the sequence listed. Read a few verses before and after the Scriptures for greater understanding, and ask God for His help in understanding each one.

1. Realize that no one is good enough. As the Scripture says, *No one is good-not even one* (Romans 3:10). *For all have sinned: all fall short of God's glorious standard. Yet now God in his gracious kindness declares us not guilty. He has done this through Christ Jesus, who has freed us by taking away our sins* (Romans 3:23-24).

2. Begin with an acknowledgement of your need. The self-sufficient think they have no use for a Savior. Jesus Himself said, *I have come to call sinners, not those who <u>think</u> they are already good enough* (Mark 2:17). If you recognize your own deficiency, if you can see places where the disease of sin has established a hold over your life, you are already headed in the right direction.

3. Understand that God loves you, even through you are a sinner. Consider this: *But God showed his great love for us by sending Christ to die for us while we were still sinners* (Romans 5:8). *For God so loved the world that he gave his only Son, so that everyone who believes in him will not perish but have eternal life* (John 3:16).

4. The required action – Place your faith (trust) in the Lord Jesus Christ to be forgiven. If this is the desire of your heart, try talking to God in simple words like these:

Dear Lord, I know I have sinned and need your forgiveness. I believe Your Son died on the cross in my place and was raised from the dead. Please forgive me of my sins. I receive Your Son by placing faith in Him as my Savior. In Jesus Name, amen.

5. Assurance of Salvation. If this is your sincere prayer, you're a member of God's family: *If you confess with your mouth that Jesus is Lord and believe in your heart that God raised Him from the dead, **you will be saved**. For it is by believing in your heart that you are made right with God, and it is by confessing with your mouth that you are saved.* (Romans 10:9). *God saved you by his special favor when you believed. And you can't take credit for this; it is a gift from God. Salvation is not a reward for the good things we have done, so none of us can boast about it* (Ephesians 2:8-9).

6. Grow through obedience to the Bible. After salvation through faith in Christ, God wants us also to demonstrate obedience to Christ obeying what He says through His Word. Ways to grow in your relationship with Christ are to spend time in prayer, study the Scriptures and get involved with your Christian brothers and sisters. Find a local church, Bible study, or Christian support group where you can grow in fellowship with other believers. Our frequent prayer should be, "God, teach me to be obedient to all your desires for me."